LIVERPOOL TRAMWAYS

Brian P Martin

Series editor Robert J Harley

1. The Eastern Routes

MP Middleton Press

Cover Picture: Streamliner 909 stands at Pagemoss terminus in this 1956 scene. It is on route 40 ready for the 35 minute journey to the Pier Head. The former tracks to Prescot and Longview curve away in the background. (Wallasey Tramway Preservation Group)

Cover Colours: These are similar to the last Liverpool Corporation Passenger Transport livery of green and cream, which was introduced by the then new transport manager, W.M.Hall, in 1947.

To my wife Dorothy

Published November 1997

ISBN 1 901706 04 4

© Middleton Press

Design Deborah Goodridge

Published by
  Middleton Press
  Easebourne Lane
  Midhurst, West Sussex
  GU29 9AZ
Tel: 01730 813169
Fax: 01730 812601

Printed & bound by Biddles Ltd,
  Guildford and Kings Lynn

CONTENTS

INTRODUCTION AND ACKNOWLEDGEMENTS

Interest in Liverpool trams is still very much a going concern with three active local tram societies and the heritage line at Birkenhead where Liverpool trams can still be seen. It is forty years since the last tram ran in Liverpool and it is pretty safe to say that the "Green Goddess" is still remembered and revered with affection by generations of Liverpudlians. Liverpool trams are covered in the *Tramway Classics* series by dividing the city into three areas: the northern routes, the eastern routes and the routes of the south end. A fourth volume will deal with the numerous cross-city and industrial routes.

This volume concentrates on the tram routes which ran into the east side of the city, along the corridors of West Derby Road, Prescot Road and Edge Lane. Included is the excellent and interesting 49 route which ran completely in the eastern suburbs linking the south end at Penny Lane with the northern routes at Muirhead Avenue East and the East Lancashire Road. My thanks go to those whose photographs appear in this volume: R.B.Parr, H.B.Priestley and N.N.Forbes, whose collections are now part of the National Tramway Museum records, R.Dudley-Caton, J.Maher, J.A.Peden, Merseyside Tramway Preservation Society, Wallasey Tramway Preservation Group, B.Mettam,

G.E.Baddeley, J.W.Gahan, M.Rooum, R.J.S.Wiseman, R.Anderson, F.N.T.Lloyd-Jones, M.Jenkins, A.D.Packer, R.F.Mack, A.M.Gunn, R.Stephens, Dr.B.Dutton and R.W.A.Jones. Apologies to those whose pictures I have been unable to identify, some of these are entered as part of my collection. Especial sincere thanks to J.W.Gahan - the "highest authority" on Liverpool trams - to whom I always turn for information, and to A.F.Gahan for his comments and suggestions regarding the captions. I am also indebted to Terry Russell for use of the rolling stock plans.

The Ordnance Survey maps were supplied by the Liverpool Central Libraries Record Office. The map of the eastern routes is by courtesy of T.Daniel. The system map and list of tram routes are from the LCPT Transport Guide for 1947.

May I commend readers who wish to know more about Liverpool trams to read *Liverpool Transport* by J.B.Horne and T.B.Maund, *Edge Lane Roundabout* by B.P.Martin, *A Nostalgic Look at Liverpool Trams 1945-57* by S.Palmer and B.P.Martin, *Liverpool Tramways 1943-57* by R.E.Blackburn, *Liverpool Trams Fleet List* by T.J.Martin and the many volumes of pocket picture albums on Liverpool Trams published by the MTPS by T.J.Martin.

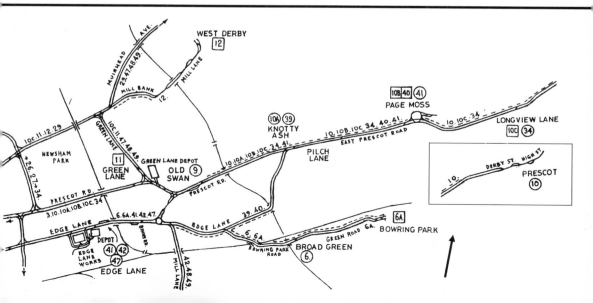

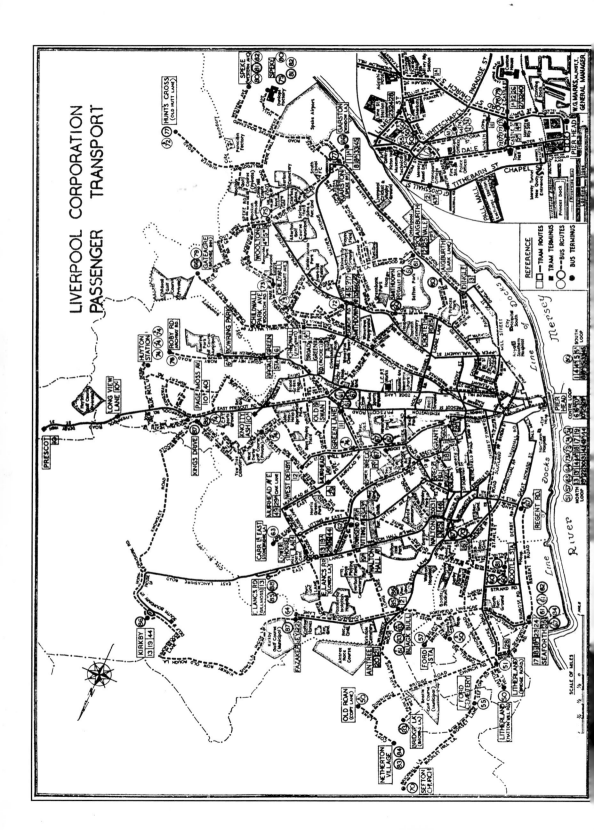

LIVERPOOL CORPORATION PASSENGER TRANSPORT

GEOGRAPHICAL SETTING

Liverpool stands on the north bank of the River Mersey at its mouth where it joins the expanse of Liverpool Bay and the Irish Sea. Formerly in Lancashire, although its cosmopolitan nature belied this fact, it is now in the County of Merseyside. The more obvious Lancashire towns of Southport, Ormskirk, Prescot, St. Helens, Warrington and Widnes closely surround Liverpool.'

The maps are from 1927 and are are at the scale of 25ins to 1 mile. North is at the top of the page, except where a bold arrow indicates otherwise.

HISTORICAL BACKGROUND

The antiquity of Liverpool goes back to Saxon times, although there is nothing existing of its most ancient buildings which included the tower and the castle, on the site of which now stands the Victoria Monument. The present oldest building dates back to 1717 - the Bluecoat Chambers. The first event of local importance was on 28th August 1207 when King John granted a charter creating Liverpool a free borough. Previously it was only a fishing village. A second charter granted by Henry III in 1229 conferred rights upon merchants the privileges of buying and selling of merchandise and of electing a mayor, sheriffs and bailiffs.

It was not until the opening up of the New World that Liverpool's pre-eminence as an Atlantic port was established. The iniquitous triangular slave trade with America and West Africa undoubtedly contributed vastly to Liverpool's wealth. The extension of the docks system in the 19th century, both northwards and southwards of the Pier Head created a need for public transport. The opening of the Liverpool and Manchester Railway (the world's first passenger line) in 1830 also created a new demand and pattern of requirements. Stagecoaches and horse buses served the docks and acted as feeders to the railway stations.

History decrees that it was the people of Birkenhead who witnessed in August 1861 the opening of Britains first street tramway. Trams appeared in Liverpool from the borough boundary at Fairfield to the Old Swan on 2nd July 1861. It was hoped to extend citywards as the tramway became accepted by its many critics and doubt-ers. However, the line was removed by 1862. Despite this setback the idea of smooth running horse trams was kept alive and in 1865 the Liverpool Tramways Co. was formed, but after laying a sample stretch of "non-obstructive" tramway in Castle Street, the company foundered and was dissolved. A new company was begun in 1868 and by the following year, tracks to Dingle and an Inner Circle were laid, the first cars running on 1st November. The horse tramways were gradually extended until being superseded by the first electric tramcars.

The Liverpool Tramways Co. was acquired by Liverpool Corporation in 1897 and soon set about electrifying the system, and the first electric trams commenced a year later. These pioneer vehicles were German built Altona Ringbahn single deckers with matching trailers. They opened the electric services to Dingle. The second tramway to Princes Park Gates in 1899 utilised American built single deck bogie cars known as "Philadelphias". By 1902 all the horse routes had been electrified, except for the disputed Litherland service which lingered on until August 1903. Various derivatives of open-top four wheelers built by the blossoming British tram builders, Milnes, Westinghouse and Dick, Kerr, were put into service after the early demise of the vastly unsuitable German cars.

The "Preston" type tram with a three window lower saloon became standard and later received various top covers. This style of tram later developed as the famous Liverpool Bellamy cars, and these vehicles were part of the tramway scene in the city for over a quarter of a century. Enclosed cars followed which resulted in the superb series of the 1930s when the city's tramways were modernised, culminating in the development of the ultimate Liverpool tramcar, the fine bogie streamliners of 1936. The four wheel economy version of these, the Baby Grands, lasted until the end of tramway operation. In 1953-54 a total of 46 redundant Streamliners were sold to Glasgow and they ran there until 1960.

Liverpool's tram routes at their zenith totalled 97 route miles/155kms, of which 28 miles/44kms were on reserved tracks. The tram to bus conversion programme began in June 1948 with the closure of the 26/27 Outer Circular routes. Nine years later with the last tram on the 6A and 40 routes on 14th September 1957, the process was complete.

In this volume the routes covered are:

No.	inward	outward
6	Pier Head	Broadgreen Station
6A	Pier Head	Bowring Park
9, 9A	Short workings on the Prescot Road routes.	
10	Castle Street	Prescot
10A	Pier Head	Knotty Ash
10B	Pier Head	Pagemoss
10C	Pier Head	Longview
11	North John Street	Green Lane
12	Castle Street	West Derby
29	Pier Head	East Lancashire Road
29A	North John Street	Muirhead Avenue East
29B	North John Street	Muirhead Avenue Bridge
39	Short workings of route 40	Pilch Lane
40	Pier Head	Pagemoss
41	Edge Lane	Pagemoss
42	Edge Lane	Penny Lane
47	Edge Lane	Muirhead Avenue East
48	Kirkby/Gillmoss	Penny Lane
49	Muirhead Avenue East	Penny Lane
—	Caird Street	Pagemoss

1947 Transport Guide

TRAM ROUTES

1	PENNY LANE & CITY via Garston & Aigburth	*22A	FAZAKERLEY & CITY via Hale Road
1A, 1B	GARSTON & CITY via Aigburth	23	SEAFORTH & CITY via Strand Road
*2	BLACK BULL & CITY via Walton	24	SEAFORTH & CITY via Knowsley Road
3	WALTON & DINGLE via Lime Street	25	WALTON & AIGBURTH via Moss Street
4	PENNY LANE & CITY via Wavertree	26	OUTER CIRCULAR via Oakfield Rd. & Lodge Lane
4A	CHILDWALL & CITY via Wavertree		(short journeys 26A)
4W	WOOLTON & CITY via Wavertree	27	OUTER CIRCULAR via Lodge Lane & Oakfield Rd
5	WAVERTREE & CITY via Smithdown Road		(short journeys 27A)
5A	PENNY LANE & CITY via Smithdown Road	28	LITHERLAND & CITY via Scotland Road
5W	WOOLTON & CITY via Smithdown Road	29	EAST LANCASHIRE ROAD & CITY via Tuebrook
6	BROADGREEN & CITY via Edge Lane	29A	MUIRHEAD AVENUE EAST & CITY via Tuebrook
6A	BOWRING PARK & CITY via Edge Lane	30	WALTON & CITY via Netherfield Road
*7	PENNY LANE & CITY via London Road	31	WALTON & CITY via Heyworth Street
8	AIGBURTH & CITY via Garston & Smithdown Road	*32	PENNY LANE & CITY via Park Lane
8A	GARSTON & CITY via Smithdown Road	33	GARSTON & CITY via Princes Park
*9	OLD SWAN & CITY via Kensington	*34	LONGVIEW LANE & SEAFORTH via Everton Valley
10	PRESCOT & CITY via Old Swan	*35	FAZAKERLEY & SEAFORTH via Hale Road
*10A	KNOTTY ASH & CITY via Old Swan	*36	LOWER LANE & SEAFORTH via Hale Road
10B	PAGEMOSS AVENUE & CITY via Old Swan	*37	UTTING AV. EAST & SEAFORTH via Everton Valley
10C	LONGVIEW LANE & CITY via Old Swan	*38	PENNY LANE & SEAFORTH via Heyworth Street
11	GREEN LANE & CITY via Tuebrook	*39	KNOTTY ASH & CITY via Brookside Avenue
12	WEST DERBY & CITY via Tuebrook	40	PAGEMOSS AVENUE & CITY via Brookside Ave.
13	EAST LANCS. ROAD & CITY via Townsend Lane	*41	PAGEMOSS AVENUE & EDGE LANE via Old Swan
13A	BROAD LANE & CITY via Townsend Lane	*42	PENNY LANE & EDGE LANE via Mill Lane
14	UTTING AVENUE EAST & CITY via Townsend Lane	43, 43B	UTTING AVENUE & CITY via Everton Valley
*14A	CHERRY LANE & CITY via Townsend Lane	*43A	UTTING AVENUE & CITY via Robson Street
15, 15A	CROXTETH ROAD & CITY via Princes Park	44	KIRKBY or GILLMOSS & CITY via Everton Valley
16	LITHERLAND & CITY via Vauxhall Road	44A	LOWER LANE & CITY via Everton Valley
17	SEAFORTH & CITY via Derby Road	45	PENNY LANE & CITY via Aigburth & Mill Street
18	SEAFORTH & BRECKFIELD RD. via Everton Valley	45A	GARSTON & CITY via Aigburth & Mill Street
*18A	SEAFORTH & EVERTON RD. via Everton Valley	46	PENNY LANE & WALTON via Moss Street
19	KIRKBY, HORN HOUSE LANE or GILLMOSS & CITY via Robson Street	*47	MUIRHEAD AVE. EAST & EDGE LANE
19A	LOWER LANE & CITY via Robson Street	*48	PENNY LANE & GILLMOSS or MUIRHEAD AVENUE EAST & WOOLTON
20	AINTREE & AIGBURTH via Park Road		
	(short journeys 20A)	49	PENNY LANE & MUIRHEAD AVE. EAST via Old Swan
21	AINTREE & AIGBURTH via Mill Street		
22	FAZAKERLEY & CITY via Walton Road	*	DINGLE & GILLMOSS

*Denotes Part-time Routes

EASTERN ROUTES IN THE CITY

1. Liverpool's imposing Royal Liver Building dominates the Pier Head terminus as Baby Grand 249 heads for Bowring Park. The Cunard Building can be seen on the right, whilst several Crosville buses stand time. A Lodekka is ready to depart on the 116 service to Prescot. This was the scene in 1956. (B.P.Martin)

2. This is a 1931 view of one of the Pier Head's three classic buildings - the Mersey Docks and Harbour Board's offices. One of Liverpool's ubiquitous Bellamy trams on route 11 is eclipsed by one of the new Priestly Bogie cars of the 770-781 series. The newer vehicle, which entered service that year is exhorting people to use the "new" clean electricity, while the older car invites people to HEAT BY GAS. (R.B.Parr/NTM)

3. Bound for Pagemoss, rebuilt Priestly Standard 755 is about to pass the Royal Liver Buildings at the Pier Head. The sheds of Princes Dock to the left are dwarfed by the tall warehouses on the Dock Road, near to where the Atlantic Tower Hotel is today. (R.Dudley-Caton)

4. Bellamy 145, ready with its indicator turned for its return to Knotty Ash, leads a procession of similar cars down Water Street whilst a lone cyclist avoids the tram rails. Hats seemingly are a pre-requisite for the pedestrians.
(B.P.Martin Coll.)

5. Approaching the Pier Head, Bogie Streamliner 988 traverses the canyon between the Royal Liver Buildings and the Cunard Building. With the legend THRELFALLS, the Goree Piazza stands on the Dock Road with the Tower Buildings on the left and West Africa House on the right. A Liverpool Overhead Railway train halts at the Pier Head station. Motorists of the 1952 period find it easy to park in this section of Water Street. (H.B.Priestley/NTM)

6. Liverpool Overhead Railway's Pier Head Station, the most palatial intermediate station on the line, overlooks a Baby Grand bound for the Pier Head on the 6A. In Water Street, the protruding Town Hall is visible at the top of the slope. Barker and Dobson Chocolate, a local confectionery firm, advertises on the LOR structure. (B.P.Martin Coll.)

7. Photographed from the LOR's Pier Head station in August 1955, bogie streamliner 157 threads its way down Water Street. India Buildings and West Africa House on the right form an imposing backdrop. A Jowett Bradford van has the freedom of the road. (R.B.Parr/NTM)

8. We reach Mann Island and catch a glimpse of the Overhead Railway. A Baby Grand passes Liverpool's main Austin dealers, Voss Motors, complete with an Austin Devon parked outside. Towering over all is the former Mersey Railway pumping station. The Voss premises are now occupied by Road Range, Mercedes dealers, and the pumping house is a preserved building housing modern day electric machinery. (J.A.Peden)

9. Liverpool's "other" main city centre artery, Dale Street, is viewed at the junction of North John Street. Dale Street was used by route 11 to Church Street. To the left is Rigby's Buildings. Visible by the Belisha beacon is an archway leading to a quaint byway, Leather Lane. (MTPS)

10. Passing Liverpool City Museums with its imposing corinthian columns, car 400 on the 29 descends William Brown Street bound for the Pier Head via Dale Street. To the right of the tram is the Wellington Column, whilst one of the several city branches of Burton's tailors stands on the corner of Commutation Row and London Road. (E.A.Gahan)

11. The south portico of St.George's Hall is seen from Queen Square/Roe Street, outside the Royal Court Theatre. The tram is on the crossover used by peak hour services on the 6 and 6A. Queen Square was the focal point for the wholesale fruit trade serving the nearby St.John's Market and fruiterers throughout the city. The old established Stork Hotel was also nearby. (B.P.Martin)

6
6A
6B
6C
9
9A
10
10A
10B

PRIVATE
AIGBURTH
AINTREE
FOOTBALL GROUND
OLD HAYMARKET
EDGE LANE
ST OSWALDS ST
PENNY LANE
BOWRING PARK
BROADGREEN
LONGVIEW
PAGEMOSS
OLD SWAN
PIER HEAD
CASTLE ST
NORTH JOHN ST

CLAYTON SQ
LIME ST
GREEN LANE
MUIRHEAD AV
MUIRHEAD AV EAST

12. Church Street, Liverpool's main shopping thoroughfare, is depicted in the 1920s. Motor traffic has grown necessitating a policeman on point duty at the Paradise Street/Whitechapel junction. Two distinguished looking gentlemen complete with panamas and straw hats wait to cross, or maybe to ask the policeman the way to Lime Street Station! A sandwich board advertises all wool suits at 50 shillings (£2.50) at 13 Lord Street, the premises of Fifty Shilling Tailors. To the right is a well-loved Liverpool emporium, Cooper's, a delightful delicatessen with aromas that teased the senses. (B.P.Martin Coll.)

14. Car 224 has just turned into Parker Street from Church Street and is about to approach the Clayton Square stop. Spinney House, with Littlewoods Stores below, is now completed. To the right are Reeces and Owen Owen department stores, meccas for 1950s shoppers. The bus on the left is a tram replacement on the 10 route. (J.Maher)

13. Car 167 is pictured on a quiet Sunday morning at the Church Street/Parker Street junction. Post-war reconstruction goes ahead with Littlewoods Organisation's Spinney House taking shape. The aptly named "holy" junction is seen middle distance with Coopers on the corner of Church Street and Paradise Street. The other two streets making up this spiritual crossroads are Whitechapel and Lord Street! (B.P.Martin Coll.)

ALL TRAMS INWARD
STOP
HERE

15. At the Clayton Square tram stop outside Owen Owen's, car 966 on the 40 heads for Pagemoss, whilst car 947 on the 14 service to Utting Avenue East, waits to draw up. On the left the steelwork of post-war reconstruction rises skywards. (R.B.Parr/NTM)

16. With Lime Street in the background, car 223 creeps down Elliot Street with the old St.John's Market on the left. Tram replacement 12 bus is depicted at a spot where today a flight of steps joins the two levels of this street. Excavation and levelling to facilitate the new St.John's Precinct provides a sharp contrast with this scene from tram days. (B.P.Martin)

17. We arrive at an interesting corner of the city and note Walker's hostelry, the Vines Hotel, also known as the "Big House". This building dominates the Lime Street/Copperas Hill corner. Liverpool's premier hotel, the Adelphi can be just seen on the right. The taxis are queueing up at the rank, which still exists today. Car 272 is about to turn left into Brownlow Hill on route 40 to Pagemoss. Lime Street to the left was the home of four cinemas - Scala, Futurist, Forum and the Palais de Luxe. (B.P.Martin)

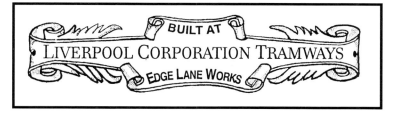

BUILT AT
LIVERPOOL CORPORATION TRAMWAYS
EDGE LANE WORKS

18. Lime Street is pictured with Lime Street Chambers, formerly the North Western Hotel, which flank the entrance to Lime Street Station. This was once the offices of the British Transport Commission which encompassed British Railways, British Road Services and British Waterways. Also visible is the row of premises, now demolished, which included the Punch & Judy Snack Bar and two Walker's pubs. Car 250 on the 6A to the Pier Head approaches the Elliot Street right turn on an August day in 1957. The front platform doors are open with just the full-up chain across, allowing cool breezes to ventilate the car. (B. P. Martin).

19. Preparations for new traffic developments after tram abandonment saw this new tramway loading island constructed in Lime Street, outside the station. Crowds of people wait to cross the station entrance, past hoardings advertising special trains to the Blackpool Illuminations. On the left is St.George's Hall complete with equestrian statue, with the Walker Art Gallery beyond. Car 203 is Bowring Park bound on the 6A. (B.P.Martin)

20. The last day of operation of trams on routes 19 and 44 was also the final day of trams along William Brown Street, Dale Street and Water Street. In the picture car 249, working to Bowring Park via Dale Street, traverses the soon to be abandoned 19 junction to the left and heads up Pembroke Place on the right. A Pier Head bound 6 via Dale Street approaches. The tower of T.J.Hughes store (still in business today) and Colliers store formed part of Liverpool's second important city centre shopping area. (B.P.Martin)

P2080/18/11
OCTOBER
1956

TRAM ROUTES

BOWRING PARK **6, 6^A** PIER HEAD

WITHDRAWAL OF
DALE STREET JOURNEYS

Commencing SUNDAY, 4th NOVEMBER, 1956

ALL TRAMS WILL BE RE-ROUTED TO AND FROM THE PIER HEAD via LIME STREET, ELLIOT STREET, CHURCH STREET, LORD STREET, and JAMES STREET.

DEPARTURE TIMES FROM PIER HEAD WILL BE ADJUSTED

FOR DETAILS SEE HANDBILL AVAILABLE AT ENQUIRY OFFICES

Liverpool Corporation Passenger Transport,
24 Hatton Garden, Liverpool 3.

'Phone CENtral 7411

W. M. HALL
General Manager

WEST DERBY ROAD ROUTES

21. Car 875 partakes of its stand time at the 11 route city terminus, North John Street. Cars on this service entered the city via Dale Street, traversed North John Street and then left the city via Church Street. The attractive Central Buildings with its ample columns was home to Baty's long-established wine merchants, today a theme bar. The relief tracks (also used for football specials) into Victoria Street are just behind the tram. (G.E.Baddeley)

23. This is a post war scene and car 322, a Lambeth Road built balcony car, waits for a single deck bus to leave its stop outside the Carlton Cinema at the Green Lane/West Derby Road junction. The tram heads for the depot with 11A on the number blind and Edge Lane on the side indicator! The bus from the Seaforth Docks, probably a 67A, has just disgorged passengers. It is an AEC Regal single decker, one of only six single deck vehicles in the fleet at the time. (E.A.Gahan)

22. One of Liverpool's famous Bellamy cars is seen on route 11 at West Derby Road on 25th April 1938. Route 11 trams travelled inwards at this time from Muirhead Avenue Bridge. On completion of the extension to Muirhead Avenue East, routes 11, 12 and 29 were reorganised into the services of later years - 11 Green Lane, 12 West Derby, and 29 East Lancashire Road with 29A to Muirhead Avenue East. The heyday of the Bellamy lasted some 25 years; they were replaced in the mid to late 1930s by the new series of trams. Car 549 was withdrawn on 8th July 1938, whilst Baby Grand 246 entered service on 9th July 1938! (H.B.Priestley/NTM)

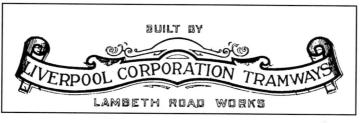

BUILT BY

LIVERPOOL CORPORATION TRAMWAYS

LAMBETH ROAD WORKS

24. West Derby village tram terminus of route 12 is seen with Bellamy 453 sporting the early type of hexagonal roller type indicator. The service number had not been allocated at this time, they were progressively introduced during 1913. (B.P.Martin Coll.)

25. Castle Street loop round the Queen Victoria Monument (now pedestrianised) was the terminus for several tram routes including the 12. James Street and Derby Square run from left to right, whilst Fenwick Street can be seen background left. Car 627 was one of 25 trams built by English Electric in 1919. They were ordered as a stop gap due to Lambeth Road works being on war-time munitions manufacture. Only eight of the series survived the Second World War to carry the green livery. This vehicle is seen in April 1947; it was withdrawn in October the following year. (J.W.Gahan)

26. Turning from a leafy Mill Lane to cross Queens Drive, the city ring road by the Jolly Miller public house, is a 12 bound for the city. A rather worse for wear streamliner car 906 is still in unrebuilt state complete with pre-war liveried cream roof, spring buffers, glass rain guards and rubber gutters. It is also sporting the long disused trafficators and painted over side indicators. The scene is shortly before conversion to buses in 1949. (N.N.Forbes/NTM)

Routes 29, 29A.
LOWERHOUSE LANE.
MUIRHEAD AVENUE—CITY

STAGE No.		STAGE No.
IN	1½d. FARES	OUT
1	Kirkby and Ainsworth Lane	12
2	Ormskirk Road and Radshaw Nook	11
3	Ainsworth Lane and Gillmoss	10
4	Radshaw Nook and Lowerhouse Lane	9

	1½d. FARES (WORKMEN'S RETURN 2d.)	
5	Gillmoss and Oak Lane	8
6	Lowerhouse Lane and Liddell Road	7
7	Oak Lane and Queens Drive	6
8	Almonds Green and Lower Breck Road	5
9	Queens Drive and Sheil Road	4
10	Lower Breck Road and Everton Road	3
11	Sheil Road and Stafford Street	2
12	Stafford Street and Pier Head	1

	2d. FARES (WORKMEN'S RETURN 3d.)	
1	Everton Road and Pier Head	1

	2½d. FARES (WORKMEN'S RETURN 4d.)	
1	Kirkby and Lower House Lane	9
2	Ainsworth Lane and Oak Lane	8
3	Radshaw Nook and Liddell Road	7
4	Gillmoss and Queens Drive	6
5	Lowerhouse Lane and Lower Breck Road	5
6	Oak Lane and Sheil Road	4
7	Almonds Green and Everton Road	3
8	Queens Drive and Stafford Street	2
9	Lower Breck Road and Pier Head	1

	3d. FARE (WORKMEN'S RETURN 5d.)	
1	Gillmoss and Everton Road	2
2	Queens Drive and Pier Head	1

	4d. FARES	
1	Kirkby and Lower Breck Road	2
2	Ormskirk Road and Pier Head	1

	4½d. FARE	
1	Kirkby and Pier Head	1

	6d. WORKMEN'S RETURN	
1	Kirkby and Liddell Road	4
2	Ainsworth Lane and Queens Drive	3
3	Radshaw Nook and Lower Breck Road	2
4	Gillmoss and Pier Head	1

27. Route 29 Pier Head to East Lancashire Road (although some drivers preferred to show Lower Lane) began at the centre loop at the Pier Head where car 961 is seen with the Cunard Building behind. Still with the original "thick" fleet numbers soon to be superseded by the Gill Sans type from 1950 onwards. (M.Rooum)

The Moss Street Junctions: Islington Square and Prescot Street/Boundary Place.

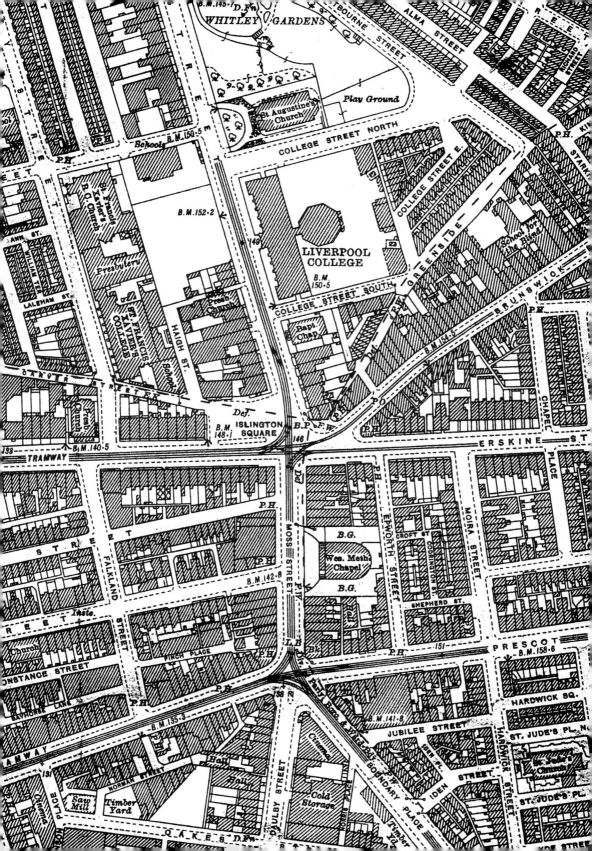

28. Leaving the city via Dale Street and Islington, route 29 trams traversed a one way system - outwards via Brunswick Road and inwards via Erskine Street. Car 902 descends Erskine Street with the Brunswick Road tracks curving off to the left. In the foreground is the Moss Street/Shaw Street/Islington junction. On the left of car 902 is a Higson's house, one of several Liverpool brewers. "Classic" motor cars also abound in this last day shot of trams on route 29.
(R.J.S.Wiseman)

29. Car 951, pictured at the top of Brunswick Road, is just about to gain access to West Derby Road, as it negotiates the Everton Road junction. The tracks to the left curve into Low Hill and Erskine Street. Most of the property in this scene has since been demolished including the well-revered Liverpool hostelry, Gregson's Well, once the haunt of local folk group The Spinners. The Ford Y on the left is displaying by today's standards a cherished number plate BED 19. (R.J.S.Wiseman)

30. West Derby Road is seen on 3rd April 1954, the last day of tram service at this location. Baby Grand car 210 heads for the city with Sheil Park to the right complete with its "temporary" pre-fabs. In the misty background rises the lofty tower of St Margaret's Anfield later destroyed in a fire. This section of road was dualled in the 1960s slum clearance.   (R.J.S.Wiseman)

The Belmont Road, West Derby Road, Sheil Road and Rocky Lane junction.

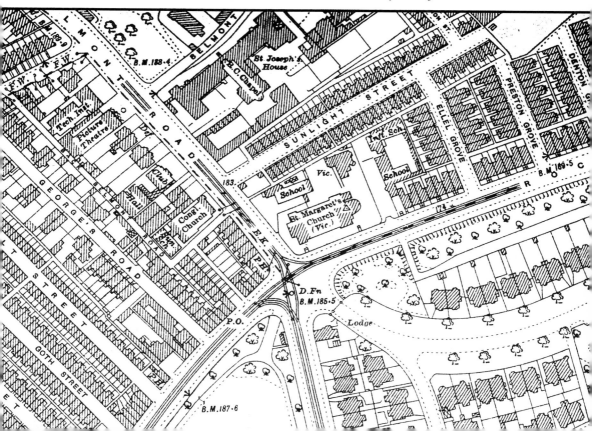

31. We proceed further down West Derby Road, again on the last day of the 29. Car 205 with the new style number blind, travels citywards; it is flanked on the left by Newsham Park, and on the right by Trinity Methodist Church at Alton Road. In the 1960s a strip of land was retrieved from the park to construct a dual carriageway. (R.J.S.Wiseman)

32. Tuebrook is crossed by the former LNWR Bootle Branch. Car 208 is about to swing its trolley sideways to duck under the low bridge. This is the last day of the 29 and car 208 displays Lower Lane on the blind. Properties on the right later suffered demolition because of road widening, whilst all the left side is still intact today. (R.J.S.Wiseman)

33. At the outward end of West Derby Road, car 911 traverses the triangular junction with Green Lane. Just emerging from Muirhead Avenue is a car on route 49, which will turn into Green Lane bound for Penny Lane. By the time of this photograph, June 1952, trams on route 12 to West Derby via Mill Bank, on the right in the distance, had been abandoned. (R.J.S.Wiseman)

34. From West Derby Road route 29 gained the wide expanse of the Muirhead Avenue reserved tracks. Here on the last day, car 901 speeds to the end of the grass tracks on its journey to the city. This car, together with car 870, was equipped with standard Priestly seats. The absence of motor traffic is evident, just a handful of cyclists have the carriageway to themselves. (B.P.Martin)

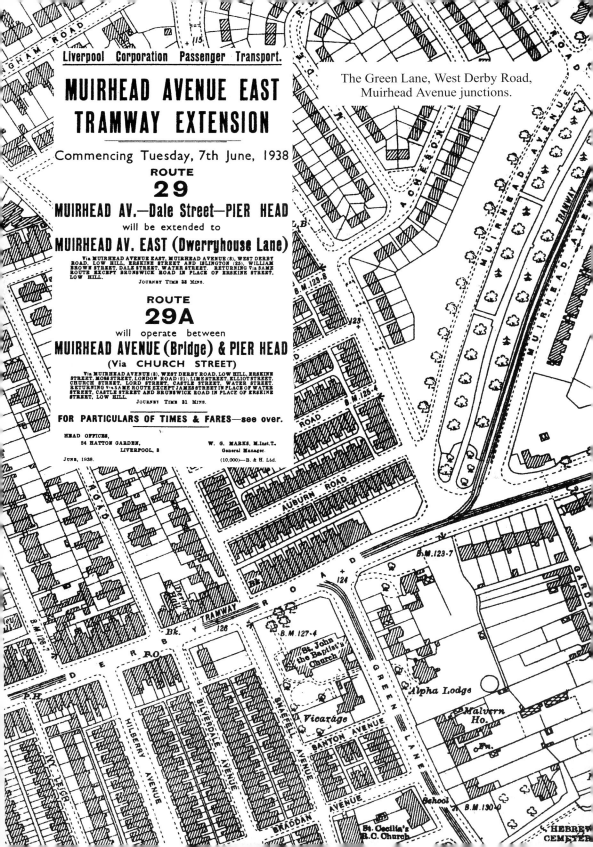

Liverpool Corporation Passenger Transport.

MUIRHEAD AVENUE EAST TRAMWAY EXTENSION

Commencing Tuesday, 7th June, 1938

ROUTE
29

MUIRHEAD AV.—Dale Street—PIER HEAD

will be extended to

MUIRHEAD AV. EAST (Dwerryhouse Lane)

Via MUIRHEAD AVENUE EAST, MUIRHEAD AVENUE (S), WEST DERBY ROAD, LOW HILL, ERSKINE STREET AND ISLINGTON (25), WILLIAM BROWN STREET, DALE STREET, WATER STREET. RETURNING Via SAME ROUTE EXCEPT BRUNSWICK ROAD IN PLACE OF ERSKINE STREET, LOW HILL.

JOURNEY TIME 25 MINS.

ROUTE
29A

will operate between

MUIRHEAD AVENUE (Bridge) & PIER HEAD
(Via CHURCH STREET)

Via MUIRHEAD AVENUE (S), WEST DERBY ROAD, LOW HILL, ERSKINE STREET, MOSS STREET, LONDON ROAD (21), LIME STREET, ELLIOT STREET, CHURCH STREET, LORD STREET, CASTLE STREET, WATER STREET. RETURNING Via SAME ROUTE EXCEPT JAMES STREET IN PLACE OF WATER STREET, CASTLE STREET AND BRUNSWICK ROAD IN PLACE OF ERSKINE STREET, LOW HILL.

JOURNEY TIME 31 MINS.

FOR PARTICULARS OF TIMES & FARES—see over.

HEAD OFFICES,
24 HATTON GARDEN,
LIVERPOOL, 3

W. G. MARKS, M.Inst.T.,
General Manager.

JUNE, 1938.

(10,000)—B. & H. Ltd.

The Green Lane, West Derby Road,
Muirhead Avenue junctions.

35. April 1938 and open vestibuled Priestly car 657 on the 11 awaits brand new car 907 as it reverses on Muirhead Avenue Bridge. Two months after this scene trams were extended further down Muirhead Avenue to Muirhead Avenue East. Until the route reorganisation trams inward showed 11 City via Dale Street and 12 City via Church Street. (H.B.Priestley/NTM)

36. Beyond the "Bridge" on the 1938 Muirhead extension at Lorenzo Drive/Almonds Green intersection, car 990 on route 29 Pier Head, crosses car 916 on the intermediate 29A service to Muirhead Avenue East. This view was taken two weeks before the closure. Car 990, on EMB HR2 bogies, was probably Liverpool's best performing tram in latter years. Note the louvre ventilators over the top deck front window; these were not fitted to the earlier batches of bogie streamliners. (R.J.S.Wiseman)

37. Last day of the 29 as car 902 arrives at the Muirhead Avenue East terminus after traversing Lower House Lane and Dwerryhouse Lane from East Lancashire Road. A goodly number of prospective passengers await to board whilst Baby Grand car 273 enjoys a lay over, before using the crossover. Car 273 had travelled outwards as a 29A and has turned its indicators to 29 to return to the city - 29A on the blind inwards signified short workings, mostly peak hour cars to North John Street. (R.J.S.Wiseman)

38. Beyond Muirhead Avenue East the 29 turned into Dwerryhouse Lane and came to the junction of Lower House Lane and Utting Avenue East - the terminus of tram route 14. Here there was a spacious triangular junction. Route 29 trams continued ahead. A Priestly EMB standard car is approaching in this 1949 scene. A new road today leads off to the right to connect the pre-war Corporation estates with the post-war estates of Croxteth. (H.B.Priestley/NTM)

39. At the end of Lower House Lane route 29 trams gained access to Lower House Lane/East Lancashire Road roundabout, where the terminus, complete with bundy clock, was situated on the start of the reserved track. Tram route 13 also terminated here, but on the citywards reservation where it ran via Townsend Avenue and Breck Road to the Pier Head. It is the last day of the 29 and Baby Grand car 208 stands at the terminus alongside streamliner 891 - the eventual last 29 tram that very evening! (B.P.Martin)

40. Green Lane, a thoroughfare which connects West Derby Road and Prescot Road, saw trams on routes 11 and 49 supplemented by peak services 47 and 48. Celebrity tram Bellamy 544 is seen passing Russian Drive on a Penny Lane bound 48 from Kirkby or Gillmoss, not long after the Green Lane Depot fire of November 1947. Behind the tram can be seen a Birmingham bus, one of the many drafted in on loan to make up for the loss of 66 trams in the fire. Car 544 outlived its counterparts by surviving the war and continuing in passenger service until July 1949. (E.A.Gahan)

41. The Prescot Road end of Green Lane, the terminus of the 11, is depicted during the last week of operation in July 1953. Car 889's conductor prepares to turn the trolley ready for the return to the city. On the left is the staff entrance to Green Lane Depot; the tramway entrance was to the left in Prescot Road next to the Green Lane Tavern pub (later a liquid refreshment oasis for tramway society preservationists working on Liverpool car 869!). (B.P.Martin)

Route 41.
PAGE MOSS AVENUE—SOUTHBANK ROAD.

STAGE No. IN		STAGE No. OUT
	1½d. FARES (WORKMEN'S RETURN 2d.)	
5	Page Moss Avenue and Pilch Lane ...	8
6	Finch Lane and Blackhorse Lane ...	7
7	Pilch Lane and St. Oswald Street (Edge Lane)	6
8	Blackhorse Lane and Southbank Road ...	5
	2½d. FARES (WORKMEN'S RETURN 4d.)	
5	Page Moss Avenue and St. Oswald Street 'Edge Lane) ...	5
6	Finch Lane and Southbank Road ...	4
	3d. FARE (WORKMEN'S RETURN 5d.)	
2	Page Moss Avenue and Southbank Road ...	1

42. Standard Priestly car 60 descends the single track, which has not been doubled even though the road has been widened to allow the building of St.Oswald's House on the left. In the background is Prescot Road with the attractive Martin's Bank and the ancient pub, the Roper's Arms on the corner of what was Percival Street which formerly led into Mary Adelaide Place. (B.P.Martin Coll.)

43. We arrive at the Edge Lane end of St Oswald's Street with car 992 on peak hour route 41 Pagemoss to Edge Lane. The tenements on the left and right of the picture have since been demolished. There is only one week left of trams on the 10B and 41. (B.P.Martin)

49	Penny Lane	-	Muirhead Ave East
41	Edge Lane	-	Pagemoss
47	Edge Lane	-	Muirhead Ave East
48	Penny Lane	-	Kirkby/Gillmoss

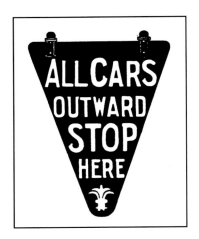

44. Edge Lane roundabout is pictured with the old Queens Arms on the left and the Hurst Gardens flats in the background. Baby Grand car 272 on the 49 will soon turn right into Mill Lane as it heads for Penny Lane. Car 179 is seen on peak hour service 42 which connected the Edge Lane industrial estate with south-end services at Penny Lane. Hurst Gardens were demolished in 1997. (R.J.S.Wiseman)

45. St Oswald's Street connected Prescot Road with Edge Lane with regular services of the 49 and peak hour 41, 47 and 48. The Prescot Road end was restricted to single track because of a bottleneck caused by Garnock Bibby rope-works. Here car 232, bound for Edge Lane on the 47 from Muirhead Avenue East, is seen on the narrow section between the rope-works and St Oswald's Church. (R.J.S.Wiseman)

Route 47.
MUIRHEAD AVENUE EAST —SOUTHBANK ROAD.

STAGE No.				STAGE No.
IN	**1½d. FARES (WORKMEN'S RETURN 2d.)**			
7	Oak Lane and Queens Drive ...	...	...	6
8	Almonds Green and Lister Drive		...	5
9	West Derby Road and Old Swan	...	...	4
10	Lister Drive and Edge Lane Drive	...	...	3
11	Old Swan and Southbank Road	...	...	2

	2½d. FARES (WORKMEN'S RETURN 4d.)			
6	Oak Lane and Old Swan	...	...	4
7	Almonds Green and Edge Lane Drive		...	3
8	West Derby Road and Southbank Road	...	2

	4d. FARE (WORKMEN'S RETURN 6d.)			
1	Oak Lane and Southbank Road	...	...	1

NOTE.
On evening journeys from Southbank Road at factory times a minimum fare of 2½d. is charged until reaching St. Oswald Street.

Routes 48, 49.
GILLMOSS—MUIRHEAD AV. EAST —PENNY LANE—WOOLTON

STAGE No.				STAGE No.
IN	**1½d. FARES (WORKMEN'S RETURN 2d.)**			**OUT**
5	Gillmoss and Oak Lane	...	...	8
6	Lowerhouse Lane and Liddell Road	...	...	7
7	Oak Lane and Queen's Drive...		...	6
8	Almonds Green and Lister Drive	...	...	5
				IN
9	West Derby Road and Old Swan	...	...	8

Routes 48, 49—Cont. 1½d. FARES (Workmen's Return 2d.)

OUT				
3	Lister Drive and Mill Lane (Edge Lane Drive)		7
4	Old Swan and Wavertree Clock Tower	...	6
5	Mill Lane (Edge Lane Drive) and Penny Lane		5
6	Wavertree Clock Tower and Cromptons Lane		4
7	Penny Lane and Yewtree Road	...	...	3
8	Cromptons Lane and Hillfoot Road ...	...	2
9	Yewtree Road and Woolton ...	...	...	1

IN	**2½d. FARES (WORKMEN'S RETURN 4d.)**			**OUT**
4	Gillmoss and Queen's Drive ...	...	...	6
5	Lowerhouse Lane and Lister Drive ...	...	5
6	Oak Lane and Old Swan	...	...	4
7	Almonds Green and Mill Lane (Edge Lane Drive)		3
8	West Derby Road and Wavertree Clock Tower	2
9	Lister Drive and Penny Lane	...	...	1
OUT				**IN**
3	Old Swan and Cromptons Lane	...	...	4
4	Mill Lane (Edge Lane Drive) and Yewtree Road ...		3
5	Wavertree Clock Tower and Hillfoot Road ...		2
6	Penny Lane and Woolton	...	...	1

IN	**4d. FARES**			**OUT**
1	Gillmoss and Penny Lane	...	...	2
2	Oak Lane and Woolton	...	...	1

IN	**WORKMEN'S RETURN 6d.**			**OUT**
1	Gillmoss and Old Swan	...	...	3
2	Lowerhouse Lane and Mill Lane (Edge Lane Drive)		2
3	Oak Lane and Penny Lane	...	...	1
OUT				**IN**
1	West Derby Road and Cromptons Lane	...	3
2	Lister Drive and Yewtree Road	...	...	2
3	Green Lane (Prescot Road) and Woolton ...	1

46. The Edge Lane end of St Oswald's Street was reconstructed in 1944 and in 1950 it was joined up with a new roundabout comprising tracks laid in asphalt with centre islands and centre brackets. St Oswald's Gardens were demolished in 1996/7. Passing local pawnbrokers Rotherham's is a battered car 287 on the 48 from Gillmoss or Kirkby to Penny Lane. This tram was the last to be rebuilt, it re-entered service in June 1954. (R.J.S.Wiseman)

47. Car 343 is ready to navigate the turning circle in Penny Lane and is travelling to Muirhead Avenue. This was the southern end of route 49 where connections could be made with routes 4, 4A, 4W, 5, 5A, 5W, 7, 8 and 32. This tram was built in 1932 and refurbished in 1936 with EMB trucks. It was also "Pulmanised", receiving transverse seats, modern panelled interior and ventilators. Note the trafficators and power brake triangle on the dash. The imposing facade to the left is the Welsh Presbyterian Church. (H.B.Priestley/NTM)

48. This is the last day of the 49 and car 205 arrives at Penny Lane terminus and passes Prince Alfred Road Depot. At this time it was closed to trams and route 49 was worked from Edge Lane. On the abandonment of the terminal loop, a facing crossover at the bottom of Church Road was installed so that route 49 trams could reverse. The former terminal loop was then left to the mercy of the multiplying replacing bus routes. (R.Anderson)

Prescot Road: The Holt Road and
the Sheil Road Junctions.

PRESCOT ROAD ROUTES

49. Kensington near Low Hill is depicted with one of the popular English Electrics on a peak hour extra on the 10B. Car 762 will deviate from its normal route down Prescot Street and London Road and will turn right into Low Hill and then run via Erskine Street and Islington. It will terminate at the 10B peak hour queue point at Commutation Row near to the Legs of Man pub and the Empire Theatre in Lime Street. The terraced houses and shops, left, were later replaced by maisonettes. Two Austin commercial vehicles track the tram as they pass a Vauxhall Velox. (R.J.S.Wiseman)

50. From Kensington the 10B trams then traversed Prescot Road descending the slight incline to Fairfield, with the former Stanley Station of the Bootle Branch on the right and Fairfield Sports Ground on the left. Car 944, an extra from Commutation Row, is followed by car 992, the highest numbered tram in the fleet. A St.Helens Corporation service 317 is risking overtaking two trams on the offside! The vast Newsham Park is on the right. (R.J.S.Wiseman)

51. Car 763, one of the English Electrics in original red/cream condition, has stopped outside the Cattle Market hostelry. The imposing tower is the Corporation's Stanley Abbatoir. Ahead of their time, with inside framed bogies with bevel gear monomotors, these trams proved troublesome. They were later modernised and repainted in the new green livery by the late 1930s. At this time 10A trams ran to Knotty Ash. (B.P.Martin Coll.)

52. The facade of Green Lane Depot,which was in Prescot Road, looks forlorn as 875 (soon to be sold to Glasgow) crashes over the crossings on the way to Pagemoss. Closed to trams only two months previously, Edge Lane Depot continued to run the 10B route until the last day in March 1955. The main entrance of the depot was blocked off and access for buses was gained by a new side entrance in Green Lane. It was in this depot that sister car 869 (rescued from Glasgow, where it became car 1055) was restored to Liverpool condition by the Merseyside Tramway Preservation Society with help from Merseyside Transport and the Merseyside Civic Society from 1967 to 1979. (R.J.S.Wiseman)

The Green Lane/Prescot Road junction and
Green Lane Tram Sheds.

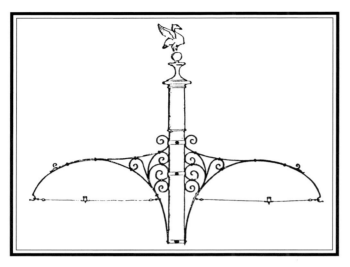

53. Always figuring in the Liverpool tramway annals is Old Swan, an important focal point on the system. Here there was a siding and to the right was the site of the old horse car depot, where Pemberton Road now stands. Bellamy cars 165, for the city, and 194, for Knotty Ash, pause at the pleasure of the inspector. The Old Swan pub still stands today, but Hoults Cash Stores to the right on the corner of St Oswald's Street was demolished in the 1930s and the road junction widened to allow the building of St Oswald's House tenements. The single track layout remained in the original part of the street. (B.P.Martin Coll.)

54. Car 906 is seen on Prescot Road en route to Pagemoss near the Queens Drive crossing. Here is the Black Horse pub, and the siding where 9 and 9A trams used to turn. On the left is George Sturla's "check" stores and on the right side the art deco Curzon Cinema built in 1936 with its attendant row of shops including a branch of Woolworth's. Local film-makers Ron and Frank Oldfield made a last week souvenir film of the Prescot Road trams and entitled it *The Black Horse Will Always Remember*. (R.J.S.Wiseman)

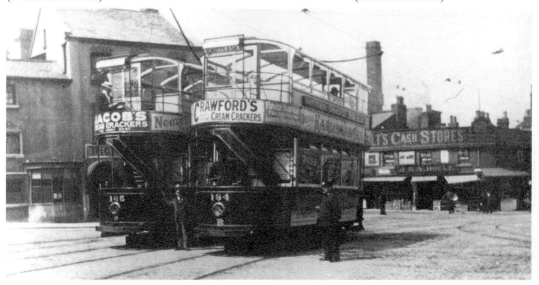

55. Next stop from Queens Drive is Knotty Ash Station on the Cheshire Lines Railway which tunnels under East Prescot Road at this point. Car 950, which was in appalling condition in its last years, is travelling towards Pagemoss. The only road traffic in the picture is a Leyland forward control lorry in the bright red livery of the nationalised British Road Services. (R.J.S.Wiseman)

Knotty Ash showing
the original tracks.

56. At Pilch Lane crossover car 916, Pier Head bound, has just changed the points for the straight; his trolley is just on the overhead wire skate. Here trams on route 40 turned off into Brookside Avenue. In the early 1930s trams to Knotty Ash turned left off the main line to a terminus on the old road to Prescot. Post war pre-fabs are evident, whilst to the right of the bus is the Harold Davies Baths (now demolished) and Calvary Church. (H.B.Priestley/NTM)

57. Further outwards on East Prescot Road is Dovecot, but on the tram system it was known as Finch Lane. To the left was the site of the Liverpool Tramways Athletic Grounds. At the end of the graceful shopping arcade was the Granada cinema. Car 762 (now preserved and restored by the MTPS on the Birkenhead Heritage Tramway) has its trolley on the connecting wire as work is in progress relaying the crossover. Although showing St.Oswald's Street on the via blind it is likely its destination will be Edge Lane Depot. (R.J.S.Wiseman)

Routes 9, 10, 10A, 10B, 10C.
PRESCOT—LONG VIEW LANE—
PAGE MOSS AV.— OLD SWAN—CITY

STAGE No. IN	1½d. FARES (WORKMEN'S RETURN 2d.)		STAGE No. OUT
1	Prescot and Long View Lane	... ...	12
2	Huyton Lane and Altmoor Road	... ...	11
3	Long View Lane and Page Moss Avenue	...	10
4	Altmoor Road and Finch Lane	...	9
5	Page Moss Avenue and Pilch Lane	... ..	8
6	Finch Lane and Blackhorse Lane	...	7
7	Pilch Lane and Broadgreen Road	... ...	6
8	Blackhorse Lane and Holland Street	... ·	5
9	Broadgreen Road and Sheil Road	... ...	4
10	Holland Street and Low Hill	... ...	3
11	Sheil Road and Stafford Street	... ...	2
12	Stafford Street and Pier Head	... ...	1

2d. FARE (WORKMEN'S RETURN 3d.)

1	Low Hill and Pier Head	... ...	1

2½d. FARES (WORKMEN'S RETURN 4d.)

1	Prescot and Page Moss Avenue	... ,..	9
2	Huyton Lane and Finch Lane	...	8
3	Long View Lane and Pilch Lane	...	7
4	Altmoor Road and Blackhorse Lane	...	6
5	Page Moss Avenue and Broadgreen Road	...	5
6	Finch Lane and Holland Street	...	4
7	Pilch Lane and Sheil Road	... ...	3
8	Blackhorse Lane and Stafford Street	...	2
9	Holland Street and Pier Head	... ...	1

3d. FARES (WORKMEN'S RETURN 5d.)

1	Prescot and Pilch Lane	... ...	3
2	Longview Lane and Low Hill	... ...	2
3	Blackhorse Lane and Pier Head	...	1

4d. FARE

1	Prescot and Pier Head	... ...	1

WORKMEN'S RETURN 6d.

1	Prescot and Broadgreen Road	... ...	2
2	Long View Lane and Pier Head	... ...	1

58. With the Pagemoss terminus in the distance, car 249 halts at Ashover Avenue on the penultimate Saturday of service 10B. The last lingering remnants of a snowfall complete a cold February scene. This car was destined to be the last 10B the following Saturday night. (B.P.Martin)

59. Pagemoss terminus included a turning circle, a crossover (seen here) and a double track siding complete with crossover and stub. Cars going through to Longview on the 10C dissected one side of the circle with no need to go round the loop. In this scene Baby Grand car 279 on route 40 takes the opportunity to reverse, leaving 916 to return to the city via the turning circle. Baby Grands were prone to controller overheating problems and drivers took every opportunity to change ends! (H.B.Priestley/NTM)

60. The end of the tracks are seen at Longview. The abandoned rails of the 10 route, which succumbed on 25 June 1949, head invitingly for Prescot. Car 897's indicators are ready for its return journey and we wait for the conductor to turn its trolley. (R.J.S.Wiseman)

61. Route 10 trams to Prescot traversed a side reservation from Longview to just beyond Brook Bridge, where they swung across to the street tracks up the incline to Prescot. Here a Priestly EMB car is seen at this point. (F.N.T.Lloyd-Jones)

62. The route into Prescot was single track with two loops, one at Derby Street, the other at High Street. Priestly EMB car 454 is seen at High Street loop almost at its journey's end. (M.Jenkins Coll.)

63. Arriving at the terminus and just about to turn into St Helens Road, a Priestly EMB Standard is on a 9A Prescot to Old Swan short working. (N.N.Forbes/NTM)

64. The terminus at Prescot for Liverpool Corporation trams was this short remnant of the Rainhill tram track in Warrington Road. A member of the St.Helens fleet is seen at the terminus on the left in St.Helens Road. On the closure of the St Helens system in 1936, Liverpool trams used the short section in St Helens Road and the Warrington Road points and track were lifted. Priestly Standard car 147 in the old livery of red/cream contrasts with car 25 of the St.Helens fleet. The Kings Arms pub has since been demolished. (A.M.Gunn)

PAGEMOSS AVENUE— CAIRD STREET

STAGE No. IN	1½d. FARES (WORKMEN'S RETURN 2d.)	STAGE No. OUT
5	Pagemoss Avenue and Pilch Lane	10
6	Finch Lane and Blackhorse Lane	9
7	Pilch Lane and Broadgreen Road	8
8	Blackhorse Lane and Lister Drive	7
9	Broadgreen Road and West Derby Road (Green Lane)	6
10	Green Lane (Prescot Road) and Lower Breck Road	5
11	Lister Drive and Sheil Road	4
12	Lower Breck Road and Caird Street	3
	2½d. FARES	
5	Pagemoss Avenue and Broadgreen Road ...	5
6	Finch Lane and Lister Drive	4
7	Pilch Lane and Lower Breck Road ...	3
8	Blackhorse Lane and Caird Street ...	2
	3d. FARE	
3	Pagemoss Avenue and Caird Street	1

65. There were two unnumbered peak hour routes in Liverpool, one was the Caird Street to Pagemoss service which served Ogden's tobaccco factory in West Derby Road. The habit of showing 10B on the blind was unofficial, but helped prospective passengers identify their tram home. In the picture Priestly Standard car 681 is seen in Green Lane near Woburn Hill; it is travelling towards the Prescot Road junction.   (N.N.Forbes/NTM)

66. Turning from Lime Street, trams going outwards on route 40 entered Brownlow Hill. Here car 271 is just about to rejoin the double tracks. Lewis's store, on the left, was rebuilt after war damage, and it is now dwarfed by the bulk of the Adelphi Hotel. Just glimpsed to the right is Parry's Bookshop, before it moved up the hill and became Blackwells. It originally served nearby Liverpool University. Finally, a butchers boy pushes his bike up the severe hill. (J.W.Martin)

67. This is the same spot as the previous picture, but we are now looking the other way, as car 240 enters the single track section hotly pursued by one of the new Bristol Lodekkas of Crosville Motor Services. Blake Street is on the left with Harford Street to the right. A classic Morris 8 car with a number plate more suited to a lorry is parked against the kerb. (R.B.Parr/NTM)

68. At the end of Brownlow Hill a sharp curve was negotiated by route 40 trams turning into Crown Street. A sign warning motor traffic can be noted. This area today is unrecognisable; all the old terraced houses and corner shops have given way to the expanding Liverpool University. (B.P.Martin)

69. Having just navigated the curve from Brownlow Hill, car 250 accelerates along Crown Street before the right turn into West Derby Street, on the outwards journey to Pagemoss. The premises of C. & V. Dieterle, purveyors of toys and fancy goods, was on the corner on the left. Crown Street today is vastly changed, all these old properties have since been pulled down. (A.D.Packer)

70. The West Derby Street/Pembroke Place end of Crown Street is shown here. This section of track was used by 40 trams travelling outwards, and 6A trams going citywards. Here car 227 heads for Pagemoss, whilst car 222 on the 6A is city bound. The other track is abandoned, just the crossings being removed; they were last used by trams on the 25 Aigburth - Walton and 46 Penny Lane - Walton. Typical of the perverse planning of the period, was the fact that the route 25 tracks were relaid, resurfaced and then abandoned in 1952, whilst trams continued to run for another 5 years on the other track! (H.B.Priestley/NTM)

71. Whilst route 40 cars turned right from Crown Street, the 6A trams curved left into Pembroke Place past the former Dental Hospital. Ahead is Boundary Place formerly used by routes 25 and 46. Just visible is the tower of Martins Bank Moss Street branch, at the end of the elegant row of terraced houses. On the left is an underground urinal complete with its gas lit illumination. Most of this scene has now vanished due to redevelopment. (A.D.Packer)

Routes 6, 6A. BOWRING PARK —BROAD GREEN—CITY

STAGE No.		STAGE No.
IN	1½d. FARES (WORKMEN'S RETURN 2d.)	OUT
1	Bowring Park and Queens Drive	7
2	Broadgreen Station and St. Oswald Street ...	6
3	Queens Drive and Southbank Road	5
4	St. Oswald Street and Durning Road... ...	4
5	Milton Road and Edge Hill Church ...	3
6	Durning Road and Monument Place... ...	2
7	Monument Place and Pier Head	1
	2d. FARE (WORKMEN'S RETURN 3d.)	
1	Edge Hill Church and Pier Head	1
	2½d. FARES (WORKMEN'S RETURN 4d.)	
1	Bowring Park and Southbank Road	4
2	Broadgreen Station and Durning Road ...	3
3	Queens Drive and Monument Place	2
4	Milton Road and Pier Head	1
	3d. FARES (WORKMEN'S RETURN 5d.)	
1	Bowring Park and Edge Hill Church... ...	2
2	Queens Drive and Pier Head	1
	4d. FARE (WORKMEN'S RETURN 6d.)	
1	Bowring Park and Pier Head...	1

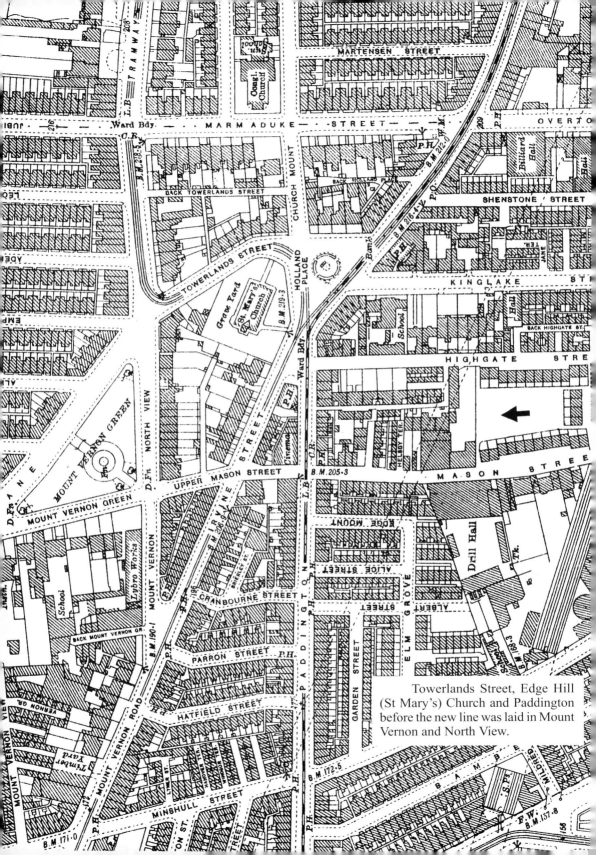

Towerlands Street, Edge Hill
(St Mary's) Church and Paddington
before the new line was laid in Mount
Vernon and North View.

72. This is the notorious Paddington, where Bellamy car 181 lost braking control and ran away to overturn at the bottom of the hill in 1934. Car 232, closely followed by a new Ford Anglia 100E, descends the inward one-way tracks. Since the 1934 accident two compulsory stops were observed over a short distance. On the corner of Bamber Street is the Paddington pub. The bombed-site is utilised by advertising hoardings for McDougall's Flour and Mackintoshes Weekend chocolates. (B.P.Martin)

73. The same location as the previous view, but this time we are looking along Paddington with the fossilised junction in the foreground. Car 242 will travel straight on via Brownlow Hill. Scores of small shops abound, dating from the pre-supermarket era; they include a record shop. Prefabs were even squeezed into a small bombed-site, whilst Bent's King Hal ale is advertised on the corner hostelry. (H.B.Priestley/NTM)

74. At the city end of Edge Lane, 6A and 40 trams negotiated a sharp curve left into Towerlands Street. The outward tracks seen here were abandoned in 1928 in favour of a more direct line via Mount Vernon and North View. The disused tracks remained in situ right to the end. (J.Maher)

75. Car 245, now preserved by the city museums, is ascending Mount Vernon to arrive at the North View tram stop before entering lengthy Edge Lane. The Lybro overalls and (later) jeans factory is on the right - all of this has since vanished. To the left is Upper Mason Street, at the Paddington end of which was the Coliseum Cinema. (J.A.Peden)

76. Car 299, the penultimate Baby Grand, takes the curves citywards between Durning Road and Marmaduke Street during the last summer of tram operation in 1957. Large villas on the left contrast with the houses on the right, which remain today. Some villas have also managed to survive to the present day, though converted into modern use as restaurants. Others were less fortunate and they were demolished to give way to offices and shops.   (B.P.Martin)

77. Car 299 reappears, this time on a Durning Road turnback that would mop up the peak hour crowds from the 26/27 belt routes at Holt Road/Durning Road. Trams would then transport them up to the Edge Lane Industrial estates and beyond. St.Cyprian's Church tower is behind the tram. (MTPS)

78. Edge Lane is seen at Botanic Gardens with the old Tournament Hall which was the venue for military and motor shows and there was even a rifle range. The hall was destroyed and a temporary tram shed to house redundant trams was erected but it was demolished in 1928 to make a new tram depot and works on the site. (B.P.Martin Coll.)

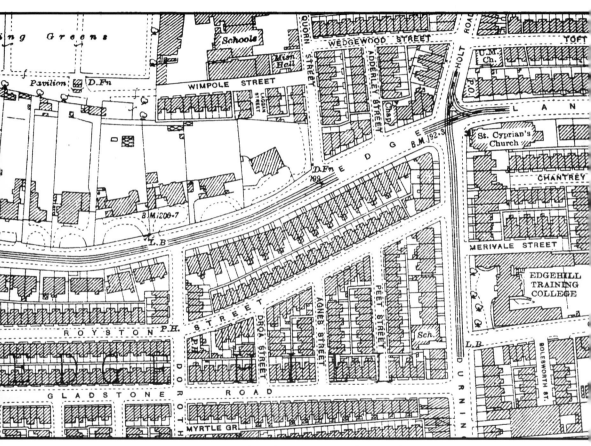

The Edge Lane, Durning Road,
Holt Road junction.

79. Thirty-four years on from the previous view, we note the art deco Littlewoods Building dominating the skyline beyond Botanic Gardens and Wavertree Park. The gardens and the lodge are unchanged even today. A Morris 8 just beats car 229 to the narrows up to Durning Road. (B.P.Martin)

80. Two 6A trams cross outside the place where they were built in 1938/39. The imposing tower of the works surmounted a vast area where all of Liverpool's trams were constructed since 1928. A suite of spacious offices fronted Edge Lane. The entrance to the traverser is seen on the right, whilst on the left is the running shed, a triangular building with a rear entrance. (B.P.Martin)

81. Edge Lane Depot and Works and the Littlewoods Pools Building provided a contrast of architectural styles. Unfortunately, Merseybus the post-deregulation successors to Liverpool Corporation, demolished this superb building and sold the site for redevelopment in Spring 1997. Always a focal point, the east entrance also served the depot and here English Electric cars 760 and 765 are seen running in, with a Baby Grand being shunted on the left up the siding. Route 39 was displayed on short workings of route 40 until March 1953, from then on every working on the route showed only 40. This was to assuage passengers who might confuse the tram with the 39A bus which was introduced on the demise of trams to Longview from Edge Lane. (R.Dudley-Caton)

The site of the original Edge Lane depot before the 1928 reconstruction.

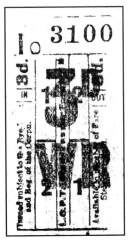

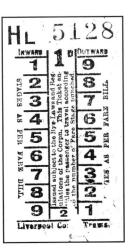

82. We can see clearly the track layout and overhead wires of the eastern junction of Edge Lane Depot and Works. Edge Lane narrowed just beyond Southbank Road (this section was widened in the 1970s) before opening out again. To the right of the depot was the Strowger Works of the the Automatic Telephone & Electric Company, now still on the site, and today known as GPT Electronics. Streamliner car 877 with blank indicators has just arrived from the direction of the city. This tram was a Garston depot car in August 1952 and was visiting the works for attention. (H.B.Priestley/NTM)

83. We now look citywards as car 966 stops short of the official tram stop for a crew change. A Crosville single decker approaches, heading for its depot further along Edge Lane at Church Road. A petrol station still stands on Laurel Road corner, whilst behind the trees stood the Convent of Adoration Reparatrice and St.Saviour's Home for Girls. (R.F.Mack)

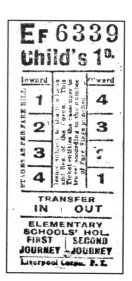

84. Edge Lane widened out at Alford Street where a siding was provided for the various peak hour services, 41, 42 and 47 etc. The now demolished St.Mark's Church was on the left. To the right stood Hanson's Dairy and further along Mac's Teashop complete with his pro-tram texts in the window. The only building surviving today is the Dryden Hotel. (B.P.Martin)

85. At the end of the siding, Priestly Standard car 21 has just left the Westbank Road stop on the 40 to Pagemoss. In the interests of brevity Page Moss Av later became Pagemoss whilst Long View Lane was shortened to Longview! Car 21 is displaying a red on white number which signified a non-Pier Head service. At this time route 40 trams terminated at Castle Street. This view dates from Autumn 1946. (N.N.Forbes/NTM)

Edge Lane at Edge Lane Station before the bridge was widened.

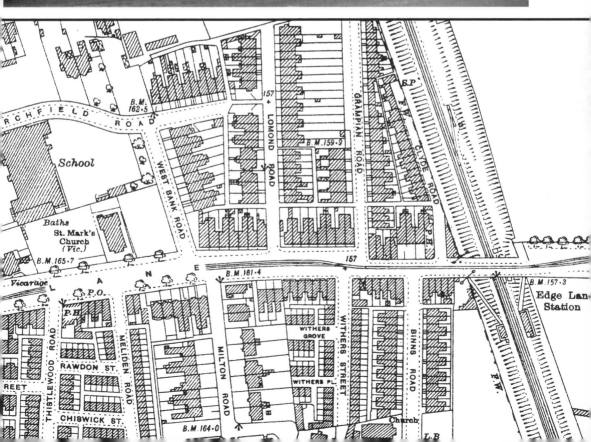

86. We view Edge Lane at Lomond Road with three trams having no other traffic to contend with. Car 214 is on a Lime Street short working, whilst the two trams behind are running in. The citybound siding is near the middle tram. The buildings to the right were subsequently demolished, but Quinn's bike shop still plies its trade today. (B.P.Martin)

87. Edge Lane at Binns Road is near where the offices and factory of Meccano were situated. A quiet Sunday morning in September 1955 was disrupted by a fire at Westbank Road. The 6A and 40 through service was suspended due to hydrant hoses across the tracks. A shuttle service ensued with 153 about to reverse over Edge Lane Bridge crossover and return to Bowring Park. One rail of the siding can just be seen behind 153. (R.Stephens)

88. Looking outwards at the same location, we note the siding and Binns Road on the right. Behind the tram the bridge over the former LNWR Bootle Branch can be seen. Edge Lane Station, was closed in May 1948. The gap between the Westbank Road and Church Road stops was one of the longest and trams would crash over Edge Lane Bridge crossover at great speed. The picture of car 263 was taken from decorated car 293 on the last day of service on 14th September 1957. (J.A.Peden)

89. Car 298 begins the climb up the slope to Edge Lane Roundabout, which was the junction with St Oswald's Street and the beginning of Edge Lane Drive. The bulk of the Pexwear factory, now an MFI warehouse, is to the right. Left is the Tapley fish and chip shop, not surprisingly on the corner of Tapley Place (now disappeared). The fencing of Brenton's sausage factory separates the chip shop from a row of terraced houses which has a pub at each end. Later in the 1960s a new palatial hostelry, the Queen of Diamonds, replaced them both. (B.P.Martin)

90. A decrepit car 175, still in pre-war livery, crosses Edge Lane/St Oswald's Street junction in pre-roundabout days. Here there was a triangular junction. Hurst Gardens is divided by the old Queen's Arms, rebuilt in 1957 and today called the Paraffin Oil Shop. The derelict mansion on the right later found itself marooned in the confines of the Corporation's City Engineers Yard, and was demolished when the new roundabout needed the extra space.
(B.P.Martin Coll.)

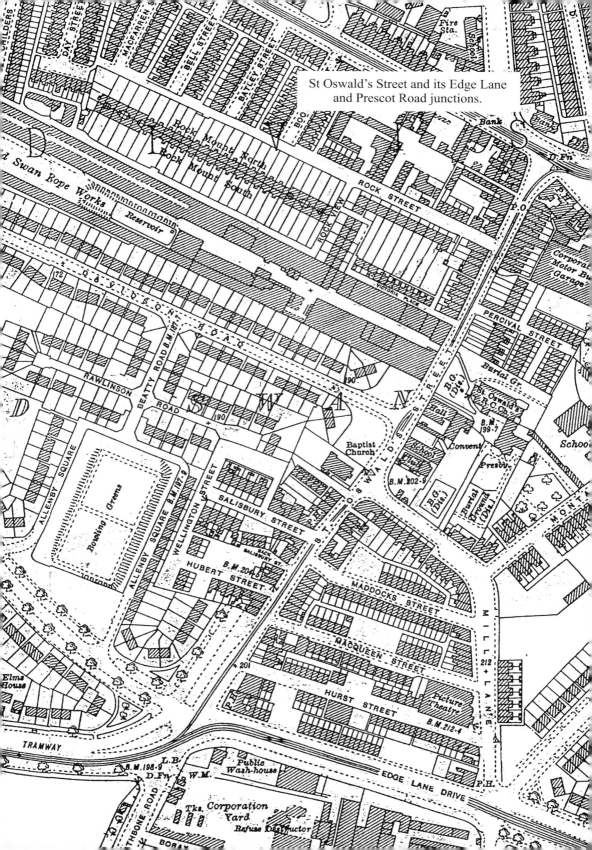

St Oswald's Street and its Edge Lane and Prescot Road junctions.

91. In 1950 a spacious roundabout was constructed at Edge Lane/St.Oswald's Street/Edge Lane Drive junction. Opportunity was taken to realign the tracks at the top of Edge Lane and to place them on a short reservation. Cabin car 792, displaced after early abandonments elsewhere in the city, found itself shedded at Edge Lane, and here negotiates the old alignment with the new tracks in place on the right. Edge Lane Recreation Ground is on the left. (B.P.Martin Coll.)

92. As the roundabout took shape, the trams kept running, albeit with some precarious temporary arrangements. Here the new curves and points are in place; whilst temporary tracks connect with the newly centralised tracks to the left. The author's childhood home is to the left of the right pole next to the now listed, but decaying, Elms House, a former mansion house, later the premises of the Youth Employment Service. (Dr.B.Dutton)

93. At the new Edge Lane Roundabout stop English Electric 767 disgorges and takes on board passengers, whilst over to the left, in St. Oswald's Street, a Baby Grand on route 49 enjoys only three more days before abandonment. (R.J.S.Wiseman)

LIVERPOOL CORPORATION PASSENGER TRANSPORT

TRAM **40** ROUTE

PAGE MOSS—CITY

REVISED SERVICE COMMENCING
MONDAY, APRIL 29th, 1957

Via EAST PRESCOT ROAD, BROOKSIDE AVENUE, EDGE LANE DRIVE,
EDGE LANE, TOWERLANDS STREET, PADDINGTON, BROWNLOW HILL,
RANELAGH STREET, CHURCH STREET, LORD STREET, JAMES STREET,
MANN ISLAND.
Returning via PARKER STREET, ELLIOT STREET, LIME STREET, instead of
Ranelagh Street, and CROWN STREET, WEST DERBY STREET, MOUNT
VERNON, IRVINE STREET, instead of Paddington.

LIVERPOOL CORPORATION PASSENGER TRANSPORT

ROUTE

PAGE MOSS **40** PIER HEAD

INCREASED SERVICE
(During Fuel Shortage)

COMMENCING
MONDAY, 10th DECEMBER, 1956

94. The Suez Crisis in November 1956, provoked by Egypt's nationalisation of the Suez Canal, caused a fuel shortage. The good effect of the crisis was that it added a few months to the life of the Liverpool tramway system. While bus services were severely curtailed, the 40 tram route enjoyed an increased service from 10th December, only reverting to its usual schedule by the end of April 1957. A few withdrawn trams were even returned to service and as can be noted here, some necessary track repairs were also carried out. Car 208 on a 10-minute service 40 is held up while the track gang repair worn curves on Edge Lane Roundabout.   (B.P.Martin)

95. Between Edge Lane Roundabout and the start of the Edge Lane reserved tracks, the first in Liverpool, was what was once Springfield Street. Hurst Gardens flats on the right and the Swan Social Club, formerly the Swan Cinema, form the backdrop for car 231 on service 40 to Pagemoss. (B.P.Martin)

96. Looking the opposite way from the last picture, we note this last day service scene with a 40 Clayton Square tram. On the right is one of the replacing buses that were introduced gradually on the last day of tram operation. The start of the reserved tracks can also be seen, as well as the former junction of the 49 into Mill Lane, which was still wired up to a feeder box at Deverell Road. Classic cars abound - a Standard, an Austin Sheerline and two Morris Minor vans are joined by a motor cycle combination. (J.A.Peden)

97. On the Edge Lane Drive reserved tracks, car 269 on a 6A to Bowring Park speeds away past a track gang relaying the inward tracks. Note the wooden sleepers which gave the reserved tracks their resilience. (H.B.Priestley/NTM)

→
98. Up the slight ascent from Sturdee Road, car 264, on a depot bound 40, accelerates along the spacious reserved tracks and road layout designed by former city engineer John Brodie, who also invented goal nets for soccer! This is a last day scene taken from the top deck of car 293, the official last tram later that fateful day 14th September 1957. (J.A.Peden)

→
99. Arriving at the Oak Vale/Broadgreen Road junction, trams on the 6A and 40 went their separate ways. Route 40 diverged to the left along the continuation of Edge Lane Drive to Thomas Lane and Brookside Avenue. Route 6A went to the right along Bowring Park Road. Here, with a month of tramway operation to go, car 288 on the 40 and car 235 on the 6A both arrive at Oak Vale to travel into the city together. Nowadays, the road to the left is curtailed, while the land in the centre is built up and the ring road's Rocket flyover dominates the background. (B.P.Martin)

→

100. Just round the curve from Oak Vale, route 6A trams crossed the Liverpool ring road, Queens Drive. Car 261 on a 6 Pier Head service via Dale Street is just about where the Queens Drive flyover is today. The row of shops on the left still stands, but the Rocket pub and other nearby property gave way to the M62 motorway link and a very complicated road junction. A new Rocket pub was built on a nearby site close to Olive Mount cutting and Broadgreen Station, former haunts of the Stephenson's Rocket on the Liverpool and Manchester Railway. (B.P.Martin)

101. The reserved tracks to Bowring Park were interrupted by two narrow overbridges. The first over the Liverpool to Manchester railway line is just about to be crossed by car 273 on a 6 Pier Head via Dale Street. Although out of view, Broadgreen Station is on the left and the Broadgreen crossover is in the background. The Lucas factory on the right was later demolished for housing. At this point today, the M62 motorway rises to cross the Broadgreen/Rocky Lane/Thomas Lane junction.
(H.B.Priestley/NTM)

→

102. We arrive at Broadgreen Station crossover. Thomas Lane is on the left, Rocky Lane is on the right and straight ahead we must pass over the Cheshire Lines Railway before re-entering the reservation. Car 241 disgorges its passengers in this sylvan scene, today denuded of this attractive foliage. (H.B.Priestley/NTM)

TRANSFER FACILITIES

AVAILABLE ON TRAM ROUTES ONLY
(until conversion to buses)

The Transfer System enables passengers to travel at a through fare to or from the City and Suburbs by a combination of two routes instead of by one through route.

The transfer must be made at a recognised transfer point by the first available tram following the one on which the ticket was issued.

Transfers operate between the places listed below and are available in either direction.

TRANSFER SYSTEM TO AND FROM CITY TERMINI

Between	First Portion of Journey Route No.	Transfer Point	Second Portion of Journey Route No.	
City and Bowring Park	40	Edge Lane Drive/ Broadgreen Road	6a	} 7d.
	6	Broadgreen Stn.	6a	
City and Page Moss	6, 6a	Edge Lane Drive/ Broadgreen Rd.	40	8d.

103. Beyond the Cheshire Lines railway bridge, a spacious dual carriageway and tramway reservation stretched all the way to the 6A terminus at Bowring Park. Opened in 1914, it saw the end of trams in 1957. By 1974 it had become the M62 motorway to Manchester, with all the cottages and houses on the outward carriageway demolished to make the concrete canyon it is today. In the picture car 268 has sped away from the Chelwood Avenue stop and is slowing to take the curves over the railway into the Broadgreen Station reserved tracks.   (H.B.Priestley/NTM)

104. From the crest of the hill at Willingdon Road near to the original site of Court Hey Methodist Church, the trams dipped down to the penultimate stop at Court Hey Road before the terminus, which can be seen in the distance. Court Hey Park is on the right whilst the ill-fated properties are seen on the left. (B.P.Martin)

105. We look from Bowring Park tram terminus towards the Court Hey Road tram stop. This scene of a spacious arterial road has now been altered drastically, with the roadway on the left now two way. The M62 would later occupy the space of the outwards carriageway and the houses and gardens right up to the Liverpool and Manchester Railway embankment. (A.D.Packer)

106. Standing at Bowring Park terminus is streamliner car 156. Today, this is right in the middle of the M62 motorway! But in 1956 it was semi-rural, the park was to the left by the trees and the waste ground on the corner of Rimmer Avenue was still undeveloped.
(Wallasey Tramcar Preservation Group)

107. Until February 1950 the terminus at Bowring Park was actually inside the Park. Originally part of ambitious plans of extensions to Huyton with route numbers 6B and 6C actually being put on some indicator blinds. The terminus was cut back to the central reservation for safety reasons. Here car 153 is about to cross from the centre island across the carriageway into the Park where there was a double crossover and a shelter.   (B.P.Martin)

108. Route 40 passed pre-war housing estates such as Dovecot. Car 272 has just traversed Finch Lane crossover. A fine arcaded shopping crescent with a community hall graced the perimeter of the estate. Spacious grassed areas gave an airy feeling to the planning. (B.P.Martin)

Routes 39, 40.
PAGE MOSS AVENUE— BROOKSIDE AVENUE— EDGE LANE—CITY.

STAGE No. IN	1½d. FARES (WORKMEN'S RETURN 2d.)	STAGE No OUT
1	Page Moss Avenue and Pilch Lane ...	8
2	Finch Lane and Queens Drive...	7
3	Pilch Lane and St. Oswald Street ...	6
4	Queens Drive and Southbank Road ...	5
5	St. Oswald Street and Durning Road...	4
6	Milton Road and Edge Hill Church ...	3
7	Durning Road and Clarence Street ...	2
8	Clarence Street and City	1

2d. FARE (WORKMEN'S RETURN 3d.)

1	Edge Hill Church and City	1

2½d. FARES (WORKMEN'S RETURN 4d.)

1	Page Moss Avenue and St. Oswald Street ...	5
2	Finch Lane and Southbank Road ...	4
3	Pilch Lane and Durning Road ...	3
4	Queens Drive and Clarence Street ...	2
5	Milton Road and City ...	1

3d. FARE (WORKMEN'S RETURN 5d.)

1	Page Moss Avenue and Edge Hill Church ...	2
2	Queens Drive and City... ...	1

4d. FARE (WORKMEN'S RETURN 6d.)

1	Page Moss Avenue and City	1

109. Further down the East Prescot Road at Pilch Lane crossover, formerly terminus of late evening 39 trams, the 40 would turn off for Brookside Avenue and Thomas Lane towards Oak Vale where it joined up with the 6A. On the left, still with tram poles and span wires is the old Knotty Ash stub terminus, superseded by new direct tracks and a crossover. The open space behind was claimed for pre-fab housing, whilst in the distance was the ground of Liverpool's short-lived rugby league club, Liverpool City. (R.W.A.Jones)

111. At the end of Thomas Lane the 40 tracks curved right into Edge Lane Drive. The roadway ahead, Thingwall Hall Drive and Campbell Drive, was the projected location of a tramway extension, but plans were scuppered by local objectors. This would have been a more direct line, meeting the East Prescot Road at Dovecot/Finch Lane. Pictured is streamliner car 869 on temporary loan to Edge Lane Depot. This tram was sold to Glasgow in 1954 and bought for preservation by the Liverpool University Public Transport Society. The bodywork of this car was later restored in Green Lane Depot by the Merseyside Tramway Preservation Society; the mechanical and electrical restoration took place at the National Tramway Museum in Crich, Derbyshire, where car 869 is now running in service. (B.P.Martin Coll.)

110. In Brookside Avenue the new tracks were laid directly on a concrete base with an asphalt road surface. Baby Grand car 299 maintains its speed over the superb tracks along this thoroughfare. Thomas Lane lies beyond. (MTPS)

FINALE - THE LAST DAY

Liverpool's *Last Tram*

SATURDAY
SEPTEMBER
14th

THE LAST TRAM WILL LEAVE PIER HEAD AT 5·55 p.m. TRAVELLING VIA
LORD ST., CHURCH ST., LIME ST., LONDON RD., PEMBROKE PL., EDGE LA.,
BOWRING PARK RD., TO BOWRING PARK AND THEN RETURN TO THE
EDGE LANE DEPOT AT APPROXIMATELY 6·45 P.M.
• INTERESTING ILLUSTRATED HISTORY ON SALE — PRICE 6d.

112. This last day scene of car 264 turning from Church Street into Parker Street was taken from the top deck of an inbound car. It is Saturday morning busy with shoppers and four of the more "flexible" buses are causing congestion, aided and abetted by motor cars. Today this area is pedestrianised and passengers have to walk to Queen Square or Ranelagh Street for their buses. (J.Maher)

113. The last tram procession is seen in Lime Street. Led by a festooned car 210, with cream painted car 293 bringing up the rear, thirteen trams departed from the Pier Head to trundle their last forlorn journey to Bowring Park and back to the sheds at Edge Lane. The bulk of Lime Street Chambers on the left is now John Moores University students accommodation. (B.P.Martin Coll.)

114. On its farewell journey, one of the last cars passes Edge Lane Works. A convoy of bikes and motor cars followed the last trams on this sad, nostalgic occasion. (B.P.Martin)

115. The last tram carrying civic dignitaries passes the author's childhood home - a very poignant moment. People look on as the procession snakes round the roundabout at Edge Lane. (B.P.Martin)

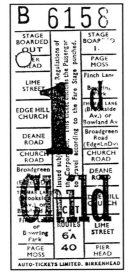

TRAM ROUTES 6, 6A, 40.

———

Replacement Arrangements

Saturday, 14th September, 1957.

———

After the morning peak and during the afternoon, buses will gradually replace the trams on the Bowring Park and Page Moss services. The last 6A tram in normal service will be the 1-53 p.m. from the Pier Head, departing Bowring Park for Edge Lane depot at 2-36 p.m. ; the last 40 tram in service will leave the Pier Head at 3-58 p.m. and depart Page Moss for Edge Lane at 4-40 p.m.

The buses will in all cases take over from trams at the outer terminals, i.e., Bowring Park and Page Moss, and will observe the tram routes and stops.

The service revisions and route alterations detailed in this booklet will take effect from the following day.

116. When the replaced trams were withdrawn they were scrapped on a four track siding, formerly a flower-bed known as "the dump". Unwired trams were shunted on by a bamboo pole and jumper cable. Here redundant Baby Grand cars 276, 218, 212 and 251 are being laid to rest at the head of rows of trams awaiting the scrapman's torch. (B.P.Martin)

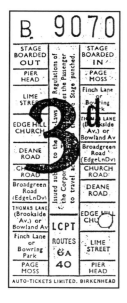

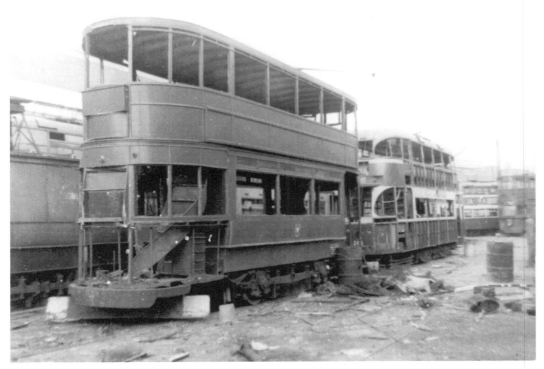

117. In 1952 the last four surviving Priestly Standards were retained and renumbered as snowploughs. Here SP4 (ex-car 646) finally meets its fate along with a works car on the left and a partially stripped Baby Grand. (B.P.Martin)

118. The shell of a Baby Grand is seen in January 1958, four months after trams last ran. The scrapmen have enjoyed an orgy of tram destruction; seats, wheelsets and bits of twisted metal are strewn across "the dump". The picked clean skeleton of the tram thrusts its trolley wirewards in defiance, but to no avail. It was the end for the trams. (B.P.Martin)

ROLLING STOCK

The English Electrics: Cars 758-769.

Although the English Electrics were to be seen all over the Liverpool system, it was the last years of tram operation that found them shedded at Edge Lane. They were veritable gems that were to be discovered running at peak hours. Because they were old trams with modern equipments, their pace and riding qualities endeared them to enthusiasts.

Numbering only 12 in the series and the first new class to be built at Edge Lane, they entered service in 1931/32. Originally they were mounted on English Electric inside-framed monomotor bogies with Peters air brakes. Electro-pneumatic control, the first on a British tram, was another innovation. They were finished in the then current livery of red and cream. After only seven years service, modifications were made to nine of the class; three (cars 758, 763 and 768) were stored in Dingle Depot virtually unaltered until they were scrapped in 1947. The last twelve bogie streamliners (cars 189-200) were not constructed, the Corporation preferring to practise economy by building four-wheeled Baby Grands. Nine of the spare equipment sets intended for cars 189-200 were utilised for the English Electrics which re-entered service between 1938 and 1944 in the new green and cream livery introduced in 1933 with the 770-781 series.

Of the nine that were modernised there were two distinct groups with minor differences. Cars 759, 761, 767 and 769 had DKB/AN controllers and slightly sloping windscreens; car 759 had ventilators instead of quarter lights and possessed a modernised lower deck interior. Car 769 had Streamliner seats. This batch of four cars was withdrawn in 1953.

The other sub series: cars 760, 762, 764, 765 and 766, were fitted with MV/AN controllers and had flush driver's windscreens. These five trams always seemed (and undoubtedly were) superior to the other four and they lasted another two years in service, being withdrawn in April 1955. The fact that 46 streamliners had been sold to Glasgow certainly prolonged their working lives. Car 766 was used on two occasions in 1954 for enthusiasts tours and thereby its notoriety lives on. Car 762 on withdrawal became a bowling green pavilion in Newsham Park until rescued by the MTPS in 1977. It is now preserved in its original condition and can be seen at the Birkenhead Heritage Tramway at Pacific Road.

The Baby Grands: Cars 201-300.

Baby Grands were to be found at most of Liverpool's depots and thus were seen all over the city. As the tram fleet contracted with just the last two depots open, Walton and Edge Lane, the remaining 84 out of a total of a 100 trams built, were shared between these sheds. Baby Grands were used for reasons of economy, and the streamlined bogie cars, expensive to operate, were then relegated to supplementary duties. However, these four wheelers were excellent, fast cars, although they were prone to overheating due to the re-use of Bellamy controllers. Because of their length on 9ft./2743mm wheelbase EMB Flexible Axle trucks, they smashed up quite a few lifeguards on the deteriorating tracks.

Although there were 100 cars in the series, only 98 actually existed at any one time. By the time the last vehicle of the class, car 300, entered service in 1942, car 225 had already been destroyed by catching fire in service in early 1942 and car 228 had sustained air raid damage in 1941.

Cars 201-210 entered service in 1937, cars 211-277 in 1938, cars 278-297 in 1939, car 298 in 1940, car 299 in January 1942 and car 300 in October 1942. Car 300 later came to grief in the 1947 Green Lane Depot fire and thus ran for only five years and one month, during a time of restricted and difficult photographic conditions. Consequently, no photographs of this vehicle exist. The other 14 cars in the series destroyed in sundry other fires and accidents were: car 209 (Woolton fire 1945), car 217 (Walton fire 1945), car 225 (fire), cars 233 and 234 (Green Lane fire), car 259 (Edge Lane collision 1945), car 281 (Robson Street fire 1945), cars 282, 290, 291, 292, 294, 295 and 300 (Green Lane fire). Car 293 became the last tram painted in a reversed green and cream livery and was preserved by the Seashore Trolley Museum in Maine, USA. Car 245 was retained by the Corporation for future inclusion in the city's transport museum gallery. It languished in the bus paint shop at Edge Lane until 1977, when it went on public display at Steamport Museum, Southport, before briefly returning to the short lived Large Objects Store at Princes Dock. It is now in store, not on public view.

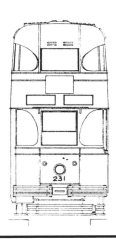

(top left)
119. In the top deck interior of Baby Grand car 248, we can note the plain light fittings, just a bare bulb in a holder. This car has been rebuilt with sliding ventilator windows. (B.P.Martin)

120. The lower deck of the same car has the fare list is displayed on the left bulkhead. On the Liverpool streamliners and Baby Grands all on could enjoy forward facing transverse seats, except for the longitudinal seats at the platform ends over the sandboxes on the lower deck. (B.P.Martin)

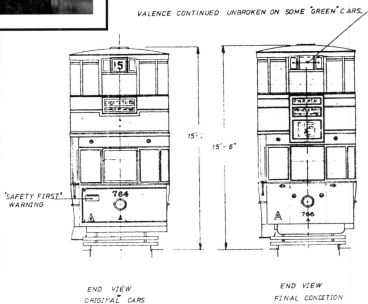

SINGLE-PIECE CURVED WINDOW FITTED AND LINE OF
VALENCE CONTINUED UNBROKEN ON SOME 'GREEN' CARS.

'SAFETY FIRST' WARNING

END VIEW
ORIGINAL CARS

END VIEW
FINAL CONDITION

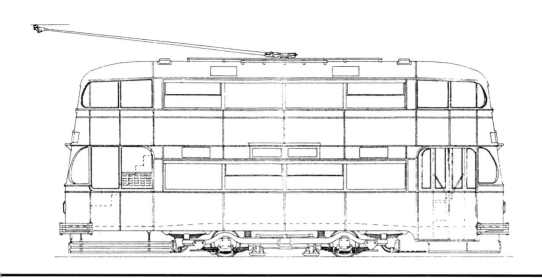

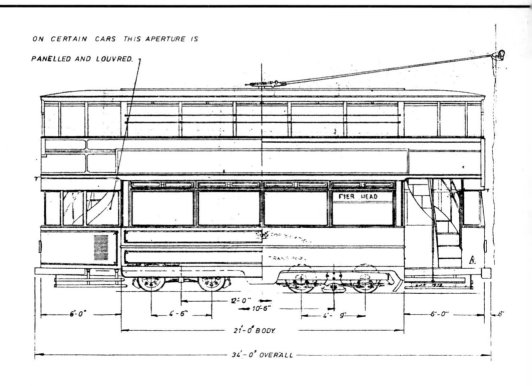

ON CERTAIN CARS THIS APERTURE IS
PANELLED AND LOUVRED.

PIER HEAD

6'-0"   4'-6"   12'-0"   4'-9"   6'-0"   6"
                 10'-6"
         21'-0" BODY.
         34'-0" OVERALL

MP Middleton Press

Easebourne Lane, Midhurst, West Sussex. GU29 9AZ Tel: 01730 813169 Fax: 01730 812601
... WRITE OR PHONE FOR OUR LATEST LIST ...

BRANCH LINES
Branch Line to Allhallows
Branch Lines to Alton
Branch Lines around Ascot
Branch Line to Ashburton
Branch Lines around Bodmin
Branch Line to Bude
Branch Lines around Canterbury
Branch Line to Cheddar
Branch Lines to East Grinstead
Branch Lines to Effingham Junction
Branch Line to Fairford
Branch Line to Hawkhurst
Branch Line to Hayling
Branch Lines to Horsham
Branch Line to Ilfracombe
Branch Lines to Longmoor
Branch Line to Lyme Regis
Branch Line to Lynton
Branch Lines around Midhurst
Branch Line to Minehead
Branch Lines to Newport (IOW)
Branch Line to Padstow
Branch Lines around Plymouth
Branch Lines around Portmadoc 1923-46
Branch Lines around Porthmadog 1954-94
Branch Lines to Seaton & Sidmouth
Branch Line to Selsey
Branch Lines around Sheerness
Branch Line to Southwold
Branch Line to Swanage
Branch Line to Tenterden
Branch Lines to Torrington
Branch Line to Upwell
Branch Lines around Wimborne
Branch Lines around Wisbech

SOUTH COAST RAILWAYS
Ashford to Dover
Brighton to Eastbourne
Chichester to Portsmouth
Dover to Ramsgate
Portsmouth to Southampton
Ryde to Ventnor
Worthing to Chichester

SOUTHERN MAIN LINES
Bromley South to Rochester
Charing Cross to Orpington
Crawley to Littlehampton
Dartford to Sittingbourne
East Croydon to Three Bridges
Epsom to Horsham
Exeter to Barnstaple
Exeter to Tavistock
Faversham to Dover
Haywards Heath to Seaford
London Bridge to East Croydon
Orpington to Tonbridge
Sittingbourne to Ramsgate
Swanley to Ashford
Tavistock to Plymouth
Victoria to Bromley South
Waterloo to Windsor

Woking to Portsmouth
Woking to Southampton
Yeovil to Exeter

COUNTRY RAILWAY ROUTES
Bath to Evercreech Junction
Bournemouth to Evercreech Jn.
Burnham to Evercreech Junction
Croydon to East Grinstead
East Kent Light Railway
Fareham to Salisbury
Frome to Bristol
Guildford to Redhill
Porthmadog to Blaenau
Reading to Basingstoke
Reading to Guildford
Redhill to Ashford
Salisbury to Westbury
Strood to Paddock Wood
Taunton to Barnstaple
Westbury to Bath
Woking to Alton
Yeovil to Dorchester

GREAT RAILWAY ERAS
Ashford from Steam to Eurostar
Festiniog in the Fifties
Festiniog in the Sixties

LONDON SUBURBAN RAILWAYS
Caterham and Tattenham Corner
Clapham Jn. to Beckenham Jn.
Crystal Palace and Catford Loop
East London Line
Finsbury Park to Alexandra Palace
Holborn Viaduct to Lewisham
Lines around Wimbledon
London Bridge to Addiscombe
Mitcham Junction Lines
North London Line
South London Line
West Croydon to Epsom
West London Line
Willesden Junction to Richmond
Wimbledon to Epsom

STEAM PHOTOGRAPHERS
O.J.Morris's Southern Railways 1919-59

STEAMING THROUGH
Steaming through Cornwall
Steaming through East Sussex
Steaming through the Isle of Wight
Steaming through Kent
Steaming through West Hants
Steaming through West Sussex

TRAMWAY CLASSICS
Aldgate & Stepney Tramways
Barnet & Finchley Tramways
Bath Tramways
Bournemouth & Poole Tramways
Brighton's Tramways
Bristol's Tramways

Camberwell & W.Norwood Tramways
Croydon's Tramways
Clapham & Streatham Tramways
Dover's Tramways
East Ham & West Ham Tramways
Eltham & Woolwich Tramways
Embankment & Waterloo Tramways
Enfield & Wood Green Tramways
Exeter & Taunton Tramways
Gosport & Horndean Tramways
Greenwich & Dartford Tramways
Hampstead & Highgate Tramways
Hastings Tramways
Holborn & Finsbury Tramways
Ilford & Barking Tramways
Kingston & Wimbledon Tramways
Lewisham & Catford Tramways
Liverpool Tramways 1. Eastern Routes
Maidstone & Chatham Tramways
North Kent Tramways
Portsmouth's Tramways
Reading Tramways
Seaton & Eastbourne Tramways
Southampton Tramways
Southend-on-sea Tramways
Southwark & Deptford Tramways
Stamford Hill Tramways
Thanet's Tramways
Victoria & Lambeth Tramways
Walthamstow & Leyton Tramways
Wandsworth & Battersea Tramways

TROLLEYBUS CLASSICS
Croydon's Trolleybuses
Hastings Trolleybuses
Maidstone Trolleybuses
Reading Trolleybuses
Woolwich & Dartford Trolleybuses

WATERWAY ALBUMS
Hampshire Waterways
Kent and East Sussex Waterways
London's Lost Route to the Sea
London to Portsmouth Waterway
Surrey Waterways

MILITARY BOOKS
Battle over Portsmouth
Battle over Sussex 1940
Blitz over Sussex 1941-42
Bombers over Sussex 1943-45
Bognor at War
Military Defence of West Sussex
Secret Sussex Resistance

OTHER BOOKS
Brickmaking in Sussex
Garraway Father & Son
Index to all Stations
Industrial Railways of the South East
London Chatham & Dover Railway

SOUTHERN RAILWAY VIDEO
War on the Line